The Magic of Writing Things Down

Sallyann Sheridan & Mary Wood

Pen Press Publishers Ltd

Published in Great Britain by
Pen Press Publishers Ltd
39–41, North Road
Islington
London N7 9DP

ISBN 1-905203-05-5

Cover design by Jacqueline Abromeit

Foreword

Things written down magically seem more concrete, attainable, within reach! Journals, diaries, lists, affirmations, letters – especially sitting down and writing a letter to yourself – works every time. They bring thoughts and aspirations to life and the vague and intangible within your grasp. And this useful book shows you how. I LOVE IT!

I am delighted to write this foreword for Sallyann and Mary's book. You see, I have always written things down, from being a young grammar school boy, a teacher, a headmaster, when studying for my PhD, through to now, an ancient being, learning scripts for my TV and radio shows. I have found that writing things down always make them clearer, more focused and easier to grasp.

All good things

Paul Darby

TV's Feng Shui Doctor and Meditation Guru

This book is dedicated to our dear friend
Christina Waugh.
"She turned her face to the sun
And let the shadows fall behind her."

Contents

How To Gain The Most From This Book

You don't need to be a writer to experience the magic that comes from writing things down. You don't even have to write or spell well. All you need do is pick up a pen and write in the ways suggested throughout this book. Tried and tested ways that have helped thousands of men, women and children improve their lives in one way or another. It doesn't matter what age you are or what you do for a living, if indeed anything. The proven concept behind this book is that writing is therapeutic. Everyone benefits from writing things down and here you'll discover some of the simplest, yet most effective ways of doing so.

Princess Diana experienced the emotional release of writing things down, Oprah Winfrey does it and Anthony Robbins recommends it as a success tool. And health specialists, including Bernie Siegel, author of the bestseller *Love, Medicine and Miracles,* recommend writing as a step towards wellness.

You've probably picked up this book for a specific reason; maybe you want to improve your personal or working relationships, feel better about your body image or be more assertive or creative. Whatever your particular challenge, by putting your heart, thoughts and voice on paper you'll discover solutions to your problems. That's because writing allows you to express and understand yourself in a way that speaking never can.

You can use it as a tool to make wellness a priority in your life too. For me, wellness is a state of mind. A contentment and peace of mind often accompanied by physical wellbeing. Wellness doesn't necessarily mean being free from illness however, as many people who have a disability or long term illness experience the joy of wellness.

The ability to enjoy inner peace and contentment, despite what's going on in your life, is a special place to arrive at. It's not about burying your head in the sand, repressing feelings or being unconcerned about people and the world around you. On the contrary, it's about doing what you can, letting go of what you can't and recognising the difference. It isn't a substitute for medical advice, nor should it be as the profession has so much to offer. This is another support, another step in taking responsibility for your overall wellbeing. If this responsibility sounds daunting, think again. Rather than being at the mercy of fate, it means you can make a positive difference to the way you view your world, the way you think, and the way you feel.

You have to help yourself though, as self-help means just that, there's no magic wand. Yet it's in this very process that you'll make the most progress, claim the most territory. That's because you put yourself in control of your own wellbeing. You take control of your own life. And in choosing to live this way, you give your body life-enhancing messages and begin to experience the joy of living in wellness.

Begin by reading the book through and see which chapters speak to you. After all, you are unique and one way of writing will undoubtedly appeal to you more than another. Some writing, such as the letters, affirmations and lists can be done as one-off exercises, whilst others, such as keeping a journal are done over time. One thing is certain, and that is that *every* exercise in *every* chapter will benefit you, and, over time, you'll have the opportunity to use them all.

Countless people have shared their writing experiences with Mary and me. They were happy and eager to do so and some are in this book. One thing that strikes people using writing in this way for the first time is the honesty with which they write and the objectivity it gives them about their life and situations. And even when they thought they didn't know what to write, as soon as they put pen to paper the words almost wrote themselves. So much so that people often look at what they've written in wonder.

Writing in this way is safe too. That's because the writing suggested in this book is between you and the page and remains unseen by anyone else and unsent. And because of this countless people have used the ideas to:

- think, feel and view life more positively

- succeed in a changing workplace

- improve relationships

- move from anger to love

- relieve stress and avoid burnout

- create affluence and gratitude

- let go of the past

- boost creativity

- enhance self-image

- enjoy wellness

- create compelling futures

Each short section is dedicated to a specific writing technique and includes tips, prompts and reveals true life examples. The joy of these uncomplicated ideas is that once read, you can use them again and again throughout your lifetime. And you can help others too by passing on the ideas to your colleagues, children, family and friends.

The great thing about using the ideas in this book is that you don't need anything other than a little time, a pen and paper and a willingness to open your heart.

With love, always

Sallyann

Unsent Letters

"I wrote 'Dear Kim,' and the rest of the letter wrote itself..."

Letter writing allows you to say all those things you've always wanted to say. It allows you to express love and anger, joy and disappointment, compassion and fear. To apologise or to confess, to say hello or goodbye, to ask for help or forgiveness. Or to say thank you.

Writing letters in this way is safe, what you write is private between you and the page. There is no comeback, no *return to sender*, no waiting for a reply to fall through the letterbox in a week's time. That's because you don't post the letters, you simply write them – it's the act of writing that's important. As you pour out your hurts, joys and innermost desires you release mental clutter and tension, draw a line under past events and create the necessary space to move forward. The space to grow, connect and remember who you really are.

The more you write, the more you learn about yourself. You discover your capacity for honesty and growth, wellness and joy, forgiveness and love. You discover that sometimes life is about being, not doing and about letting go, not clinging on. And it's here that the magic starts.

Who to Write To...

Maybe you feel let down by someone: your mother or father, lover, spouse, boss, friends or children perhaps. It doesn't matter whether it was over something that happened years ago, yesterday or this morning. Maybe you think you let yourself down by not taking an opportunity that came your way, or in handling a delicate situation badly. If so, why not write a letter to yourself? You can write to an illness too, or a part of your body that's troubling you – there are no rules. You can even write to a pet, an object or a place that has great significance in your life.

Think of someone who has played an important role in your life. Did they support you through difficult times such as an illness, divorce or job loss? Did they inspire and encourage you to believe in yourself and your ability when everyone else was urging you to play safe? Even if you thanked them at the time, you might want to do so again, you can never express too much gratitude. It could be that the person you want to write to has died – write the letter anyway. It's worth remembering that an important role doesn't necessarily mean an enormous role. It could be that a neighbour or colleague uttered a few encouraging words at a time when you needed them most. A stranger lightened your mood by giving you their smile. A cashier turned your desperately dull day into a more positive one with their refreshing banter. Why not drop them a line?

Perhaps you feel guilty over the way you treated someone in the past. You're only human after all. Now is a good time to offload what you feel about that, to admit you're not proud of your words or actions, to say sorry and to finally lay the guilt to rest.

Anger is an emotion that is certainly better out than in, so if you want to vent your spleen, write that letter. Say how you hurt, how their behaviour affected you, how it still affects you, and don't hold back. This isn't a time for delicate words and phrases; it's time to let all your pent up anger explode onto the page.

Goodbye letters can be particularly difficult to write, especially if you've been hoping things would be different. You might want to say goodbye to a child who's finally flown the nest or a former partner you've never really let go of emotionally. Maybe someone you loved died suddenly without giving you the chance to say goodbye. Now is your chance to say goodbye and express all those unsaid things.

And then, of course, there are love letters. Never forget those.

Letters of forgiveness are also special. They are special because although you may struggle more with their writing, the rewards can be life-changing. You don't have to understand why the person did what they did, or agree with it, you simply forgive – for your sake. Countless people have said how they resist writing these letters more than any other. Yet they all say that once they write letters of forgiveness they experience profound changes in the way they view the person or situation. For some it takes one letter only.

How to Start... Where to Finish

Before You Start...

As there are no rules, the following are guidelines. They're included because people who use them say they work.

Initially you will probably know exactly who you want to write to, and that's the place to start. Maybe you let someone down in the past or maybe you're angry with someone who let you down. There are countless reasons why you might want to write. And once you experience the peace of mind that comes from writing letters in this way you'll find yourself writing them again, again and again.

Write down the first thing that comes into your head. If you consider words in your mind before putting them down, you're censoring yourself, and not being truly spontaneous.

If you're writing a letter of forgiveness, it helps to quieten yourself before you write. Sit with eyes closed for a minute or two, drop your shoulders and breathe deeply, repeating the words 'I let go,' over and over in your mind.

One last thing before you start. At many workshops or training sessions we've held someone will say they don't know what to write. At a drug rehabilitation group one young man in his early twenties insisted he had no one to write to until Sallyann asked him if anyone had pressed his buttons lately. 'Oh yeah,' he said, 'but can I swear?' 'Of course,' was her response and he wrote for over fifteen minutes without lifting his pen from the paper. At another all women workshop we were fifteen minutes away from a refreshment break and Sallyann gave the group that time to write a letter. One woman insisted she didn't know what to write. Five minutes after everyone else had started she began to write. And when the rest of the group stopped for a fifteen minute break she was still writing. And when the break was over and the group returned to the room, they smiled as they watched her put her signature to a long, extremely long, letter.

How to Start…

The letters work best when they're handwritten. Somehow, the act of writing letters such as these by hand draws things out, allows you to sprawl emotionally over the page. Your handwriting isn't under scrutiny, nor is your grammar, punctuation or spelling. You can write huge letters in green felt tip, tiny words in blue ink, and litter the pages with enormous question marks and exclamation marks throughout. The letter doesn't have to make sense either, it can be a series of words – sentiments, endearments or swear words – according to how you feel. It might just be a single sentence. And if you feel resistance, write anyway, and see what comes out. Remember, this never goes any further; it's between you and the page.

When you've said everything you want to say, sign it. A large 'yes, this is me' signature if you wish. And if you think of more, add a PS or two, or five, as many as you want. So:

- think of someone you want to write to.

- write your letter. Fast or slow, in pencil or ink. Leave no holds barred. Tell it how it is from your point of view. Put the contents of your heart and soul onto this page or pages. Pour it out until you have nothing left to say.

- now sign your name. This shows you mean what you say.

Where to Finish

- you've done it! Congratulations. Now give yourself the praise you deserve.
- read it aloud to yourself. Add more if you want. Rewrite if you want, as many times as you need.

Now that you've got all that out from within, what do you do with the letter? Keep it somewhere safe? Burn it on a bonfire? Post it to yourself? Shred it into confetti like pieces and throw it high into the air? Make it into a boat and set it to sail on the ocean waves? The answer is whatever feels right for you.

You might also try responding to your letter as if you were the recipient. Imagine you wrote to your boss telling her how difficult she makes your life. Write a letter back to you from her. Go on, really get into her shoes. How does it feel to be her? What's it like from her perspective? Now write back to yourself. The key with this writing is to go to it without any preconceived ideas about how or why the person did what they did. Let the writing provide the answers. Most people are surprised at what they write here and the understanding it brings.

True Life Letters

Dear Ian

I'm so sorry for the way I treated you. You didn't deserve it. Now that I'm older and wiser I realise what an absolute bitch I was. All you did was love me, and I flirted with your friends, took you for granted and treated you like a pet dog that came when I called. I am so ashamed of the way I was, and whenever I hear 'our song' on the radio, my stomach churns with the memory of it all. I hate to think that I live in your memory as that bitch, as I surely must do. You'll never know how many times I've wished we could do it all over again. How I've wished I could contact you to apologise. But life has moved on and so have we, I don't even know where you are now. All I can say in my defence was that I was young and had no self-esteem. It was so important for me then to have men fancy me; it was the only way I felt any self-worth. All my energy was spent on having people like me, think me fanciable, and I was too selfish to consider what that was like for you. Please don't think badly of me. I now realise what a prize guy you really were and I hope you're happy because you deserve it.

Love, Sandy x

The above letter was put in a bottle and put into the sea off Teignmouth, England.

Dear Billy,

You really are a complete and utter arshole. The thought of you still fills me with rage. I stood by you through all those years of struggle. When you had no self-confidence. When you had no self-esteem. When you had no job. No talent. No money. It was me that made you believe you could be somebody. It was me that worked at two jobs so that you could go to college and learn new skills. It was me that stayed up typing your essays, reports and CVs. And for what? For you to become confident, skilled, articulate and for you to sod off to pastures new. I don't want you back, believe me. That woman deserves you. It just galls me beyond belief that after all the support I gave, you could deceive me in such a cruel and callous way. But you have to live with that, not me. It's said that what goes around, comes around. In which case you must be shitting yourself as betrayal must be hovering over your front door like a lead cloud. Here's hoping it lands.

With utter loathing, Janice

Janice says that even as she wrote this letter, she could feel a shift in the way she felt. After rereading it, she says she began to see things from a slightly different perspective. She then wrote others and finally, after numerous letters, ended with one in which she was able to forgive him and release herself from the feelings of hurt and anger. She burnt the letters ceremoniously on Guy Fawkes' Night – the anniversary of the day he left her.

Dear Immune System,

What's happened to you? Why aren't you doing your job, why have you turned against me? Have I treated you so badly? Maybe you think I should have taken more care of you. But it's bloody difficult to earn a living, take care of a family and give you the nourishment I'm told you need. Bloody difficult. Now, in this position, I feel frustrated, weak and afraid. Yes, afraid! What's going to become of us? What use am I to them now? Please, please, please start functioning better. I'll help, I promise. I'll stop ignoring you. I PROMISE.

Joe

Joe keeps this letter folded in his wallet/organiser. He says it's a stark reminder of the desperation he once felt and serves as a constant reminder to schedule balance into his life.

Prompts, Tips and Payoffs

There are many ways you can use this form of letter writing. You could set aside a regular time every day or every week, or write to a set number of people or places or things. Most likely you will write only when you have something to say or want to get someone or something off your chest.

Prompts

In case you're having trouble starting your letters, here are a few ideas of people you might want to write to:

- boss, colleague, or employer, employees
- mother, father, children, siblings, grandmother, grandfather, in-laws, step family, extended family
- friends (past and present)
- teachers, classmates
- bank manager, cashier
- husband, wife, girlfriend, boyfriend, ex-partners and spouses
- politicians, fundraisers, bureaucrats, famous people
- kind strangers, anger-inducing strangers
- pets, places and illnesses
- yourself, a part of your body

Here are a few suggestions on how you could start:

- you'll never know what a difference you made to my life
- you said three words that I'll always cherish
- I never thought I could detest anyone the way I do you
- I lied about...
- why didn't you tell me how you really felt?
- I miss you
- I love you
- did I ever say thank you for...?
- can we start again?
- why the ******* did I ever listen to a ******* like you (fill in the blanks!)
- what am I supposed to do now? Where do I go from here?

Tips

- even if you don't want to write, write anyway. It works
- write about what you feel, not just about what happened
- forget rules of writing. No one is going to mark this paper with a red pen because you spelt things wrong or forgot to put in a full stop or comma and you don't need to correct it either!
- write about things that frighten or worry you
- you can start and finish your letters with whatever you choose – Dear John, Dear Jerk, Yours Wounded, Love Sandra – or you can leave this bit blank
- sign the letter with your name
- try writing on different paper, with different coloured pens or pencils
- try writing in different places. In your bedroom, sitting room, or outside in a forest or sat in your car in a car park
- try writing at different times of the day, early morning, dusk, midnight
- try propping a photograph of the person or place you're writing to in front of you as you write
- try reciting the letter out loud as you write or whisper or scream the words if that feels right
- try something original

The Payoff

Writing about your emotions will help prevent illness, dissipate anger and ease depression. In one reported study, for example, a group of unemployed engineers who wrote about how they felt after losing their jobs were more successful in finding new ones than those who didn't. That's because they'd already expressed their anger onto the page and didn't allow it to come through in job interviews.

So often in everyday situations we hear people say, 'I was so angry, I wrote a letter.' When we ask what happened, they invariably say, 'Oh, I didn't send it.' Why not? Because, they say, they felt better after writing it, or the moment had passed, or on reflection it didn't seem worth sending. In other words, they'd written their anger out!

Sometimes you'll find this sort of letter writing painful, but that's the point. Please write about what you feel resistance to. By moving through those feelings instead of ignoring them and leaving them festering away from the inside, you release what needs to be released. That sense of relief is tremendous and you'll discover that you've created a space within yourself that can be filled anew. And this time you can choose to fill it with joy, enthusiasm and love.

Journaling Journey

*"There is a part of you which knows all and
when you give it a chance to communicate it does".*

Everyone we have ever met who regularly writes a journal say
they benefit from doing so. *Everyone.* Journaling is the name
given to the habit of writing in a journal, daily. Unlike diary
writing, journaling isn't a record of your daily activities. It's
more an outpouring of the *real* you. The *you* that is all too
often covered over by the challenges, chores and chaos of
daily life. Journaling is shown to help in many ways. It aids
creativity; can be a source of reflection, and helps you get
innermost thoughts and feelings out from within. Journaling
allows you to gain a fresh perspective on people, events and
yourself. Somehow it allows you to access your inner wisdom
instead of responding from your logical, so-called realistic
self. And, as this chapter reveals, journaling can be life
changing.

   As with writing unsent letters, journal writing is something
you do for yourself. Your journal is not for public
consumption so keep it somewhere private if you can't
guarantee others won't read it when you're not around. This
allows you to write freely and not to censor your views,
thoughts and feelings. And don't 'mistakenly' leave your
journal where you know prying eyes will find it as a way of
hurting or playing around with someone's feelings. Let's be
grown up about this!

When and What to Write

Some people choose to write in a lined exercise book, others a
specially chosen book with beautiful covers which appeals to

their senses. If you choose the latter, select a book which reflects you and your personality. Mary writes in a handmade silk-bound book, which lives in its own silk drawstring bag; a gift from her daughter. Or you might decorate a plain book with images cut from magazines – cats, cherubs, cars, a musical score – anything that appeals to you and your personality. Alternatively, decorate it with a selection from the wide range of stickers and decoupage kits available. Some find a spiral bound book easier to write in, others write on loose-leaf sheets and store them in a decorated folder or binder. Give the same consideration to your pen too. Don't compromise – unless it's upwards! The choices are yours. All we suggest is that you have a journal and pen that pleases you as a sign of how much you value yourself.

Occasionally, people find it difficult to write fluidly in a beautiful journal. They're afraid to mess it up, have crossings out, all those no-no's that still hang over from school days, so they deliberate over what they write, how neat it looks and punctuation and grammar. If this is you, start journaling with a jotter or exercise book. But remember, this isn't about doing your *best work*. You're in charge now. And when you get used to writing freely without self-censorship, you'll probably decide to buy yourself the beautiful journal you saw only last week.

When to Write

Most people choose to write their journal at the start of the day, but don't limit yourself with rules. If five to ten minutes after lunch is what suits you best, do it then. Many people start writing a few minutes a day in this way and later, having reaped the benefits, make journaling a priority in their life. It is far better to write something every day at a time that suits you rather than not journal at all. This may sound obvious, but when people say they don't journal because they haven't the time in the mornings, we encourage them to write as little or as much as they can at a time of day that suits them. This immediately removes the constraints and we're often amazed (and amused) at where people choose to start journaling. As said before, once the benefits appear, people begin to spend longer at it and play around with writing at different times of day.

Some people choose to write for a set number of pages, others write for a set time. As you'd expect, different things work for different people.

Consider some of these tried and tested ways of when to journal:

- Write as soon as possible after waking before the prospect of the day ahead fills your mind with too much clutter

- Write at the end of a day

- Write for a set time limit of say, twenty minutes, then stop

- Write three pages of A4 (or equivalent) and then stop

- Split your journaling time by writing some on waking and more before retiring to bed

If you're thinking you really don't have time to write every day, all we ask is that you try it. Because once you make journaling a habit, it's a habit you won't want to break. Often, people start journaling when they face a particular challenge or to see them through difficult times. And it works. Once that period of their life is over, some choose to drop the habit, only to resume again when they're challenged afresh. But, hey, happy people journal too! And maybe a large part of why they are happy is because journaling is a great way to keep clutter out from within, to boost creativity and to access their magnificent inner resources.

What to Write

The best thing about journaling is that you can write anything. Absolutely anything. But you have to write, whether your words make sense or not. Write the first thing that comes into your mind, even if that's "I don't know what to write," or, "I'm stuck!" Write these words repeatedly if necessary, until you do know what to write; until you become unstuck. Sometimes your thoughts will rush out so fast your pen will race across the page in a desperate struggle to get them all down. Please don't stop to consider your thoughts and feelings before you commit them to paper. And certainly don't pause in an attempt to analyse or reflect on what you've written as you write. Plenty of time for this later.

Some days all you need do is open your journal, put pen to paper and it will write itself. 'Where did that come from?' you'll ask. Other days you'll start with a question, an enquiry for which you have no answer, yet by the time you've finished journaling an idea or answer has emerged. There is a part of you, which knows all and when you give it a chance to communicate it does.

- even if you don't want to write, write anyway. It works

- write about how you feel, not only about what happens

- forget about spelling, punctuation and the look of your writing

- write about things that frighten or worry you

- write about things that make you happy

How to Overcome Blocks

Blocks can occur for a variety of reasons, a common one being a fear of what will come out from within when you really start being honest about your life, your feelings and your relationships. Fantastic! That's the point; that's part of why you're doing this. And the first way to overcome a block is to write anyway.

You could choose a lead-in sentence, such as:

- what Am I Overlooking?

- what Is My Reputation? or

- I Last Laughed Out Loud When…?
  Or select a key word to prompt you, such as:

- Sex, Joy *or* Fear

Further Tips to Experiment With:

- use different coloured pens or pencils

- write at different times of the day

- write in a different place

- write about yourself in the third person (instead of: *I felt silly when I saw him there.* write: *Sarah felt silly when she saw him there*)

- write your journal as a series of letters (Dear God… perhaps)

- try something original

Don't Forget:

- use a book and pen that appeals to you – go first class!

- write daily

- don't beat yourself up if you miss a day

- there are no rules – only guidelines!

True Life Examples

Julie felt blocked one day so decided to try writing her journal as a letter. What follows is part of what she wrote:

Dear Beautiful Book

Just let me write to you and see what emerges. What is said? What I write. Confusion. To stay or to go. I look for the answer that is right. Not just for me – for Brian too. Though perhaps that's the trouble – I need to ask for me. Let others ask for themselves. Of course. This isn't being selfish. This is taking responsibility for my life and me. I am so unused to doing for me. Keep writing. Keep writing. Keep writing... though I know not what. Just keep writing across the page, line by line, spill my heart onto the page. What holds me back? Fear of seeing it on the page? That which I know I must do. What is that...?

The results of Julie's months of journaling were life changing. She says that once she began to acknowledge on paper what she truly knew in her heart it gave her the courage to act. She ended a marriage that she knew wasn't giving her or her husband the joy they deserved. Julie is now happy running her own complimentary therapy practice in the UK and remains good friends with her ex-husband.

David felt blocked, so decided to write his journal in the third person, as if he were writing about someone else. Here's an excerpt:

David felt angry most of the time. His wife and kids said he was snappy and they'd often row. Same last night, so he'd ended up watching Sky TV until the early hours drinking beer. Too many beers his wife would probably tell him again tonight. Christ! Would she ever get off his back? He dreaded the thought of another day in the office with Ken. Ken didn't pull his weight. David even *sat by Ken at lunchtime yesterday so he could broach the subject, but Ken ended up dominating the conversation by talking about the previous night's football match. F***ing Ken. He was making David's life at work a misery.*

David said that journaling in this way allowed him to view his situation as an impartial observer might and he recognised many things. Firstly, he noticed that he was angry with himself for not being assertive over the Ken issue. He saw how his frustration at himself made him angry at home which in turn led to rows. He then used the rows as an excuse to drink too much. All of which made him feel worse about himself. The good news is that David took a course on How to Handle Difficult People and resolved the Ken issue almost immediately. He says the knock on effect across the rest of his life, particularly his home life, is unbelievable, as he feels so different about himself.

At 76, for reasons he couldn't identify, Charles lost what he termed his natural optimism and do-it-now attitude. He found it a job to get up in the mornings (for what?) and began letting things such as bills and world affairs have more of an impact than usual. When his wife suggested he start journaling, he was pessimistic.

"I'm not convinced," he told her, "but I'll give it a go."

He admitted he was doing it more to keep his wife happy than because he thought it would do any good. Charles wrote first thing in the morning for at least twenty minutes. His first entry started:

I'm doing this because Mary suggested it. But then I know what Mary's suggestions are. Really they're orders couched as suggestion, ideas, anything but what they really are.

Charles said he couldn't believe what he was writing. Yet he knew it was the truth. Within a couple of weeks, Charles felt brighter. A month later, Charles said, he was more in control of his life. He'd allowed others to make decisions for him as opposed to making his own choices. This loss of control as he saw it had led to a loss of energy and joy for life. Journaling helped him change all this for the better.

Unleash Your Creativity

If you want to be more creative – journal! So many people tell us that as a result of journaling they discover a creative side to themselves that they didn't even know existed. Painting, carving, writing, quilting, photography, woodworking, sculpting, interior design are a few of the interests people have taken up as a result of journaling. One client started writing a daily journal after he was made redundant and within a month set up a workshop in his garden making and painting moulds of decorative carvings. He's now back in full-time employment, sells the moulds as a hobby, and says he feels more fulfilled than he can ever remember.

So it appears that although you might start journaling for other reasons, previously unrecognised and unleashed creativity is often an added bonus.

Confession Time!

Many writers and artists use journaling to aid creativity and Sallyann says: "I heard about the benefits of journaling long before I started writing a journal. I recommended it to clients and friends, as I knew the benefits were genuine, yet I still didn't journal. Then I decided this was ridiculous. If I were to continue to recommend it, I would at least give it a try. I chose to write in a lined spiral bound book with a glitzy cover, a gift from a friend. The results were remarkable and almost instant.

"I'd been struggling with a book outline. Every time I sat at the computer to continue work on the outline, I pressed a few keys then decided it was time to check emails, meditate, relax, or work on another project. Relaxation is good for creativity I told myself, but surely not when it replaces productivity! Yet within days of starting a journal, everything changed. I became focused, new ideas emerged and in addition to finishing the outline, I wrote half of the first chapter.

"Now, whenever possible, journaling is one of the first things I do in the morning and I start by writing *Dear Journal...* I mainly write in blue ink and as the pages of my current journal are spacious, I write two pages a day, sometimes more. Occasionally, I'll write again in the evening. And I never beat myself up if I miss days or do it differently!

"In the spirit of sharing, here's a recent section from my own journal:

...I feel connected in a way that's beautiful, indescribable. I feel so happy, so connected to everything and everyone. There are people who might live a lifetime and never feel this way. What is it that has me feeling this way? It's a pretty ordinary day, yet even as I write this I know it's not an ordinary day – how can it be? No day ever is. Every day, every moment, is precious, never let me forget that. At times like this I know everything is possible. I love the feel of this pen gliding over the page forming words almost without my help. How strange to feel so detached, yet so connected. Whenever I feel this way I don't want it to end..."

Mary says of her journaling:

"I like to meditate first thing in the morning so I tend to write my journal after lunch or supper, whichever is more convenient. I start by listing five things I am grateful for – such as the sun shining, or my friendship

with Sallyann – and because I can be very hard on myself I also write five acknowledgements to myself – such as keeping calm in busy traffic or continuing with a writing project even though I was tired. I do miss days due to other distractions, but always come back to my journaling as soon as I can."

When to Read Your Journal

If you never read any of what you've written, you will still benefit from journaling. That's because the act of getting your thoughts and feelings out of your mind and body is what counts here. And we know of several people who never revisit their writings – ever. And when one book is full they discard it and start the next. Others never read what they've written, yet hang on to the journal anyway.

Most journalers want to read what they've written. All we ask is that you please don't read what you're writing in your journal as you write. And when you've written your daily quota, put the journal away before being tempted to read what you've penned that day. Leave it unread. And if you must revisit your writings leave as long a gap as you are willing to bear – a month? Six months would be better. Yet again, there are no rules, only guidelines.

Finally

After you start journaling you'll notice changes. Some will be subtle and creep up on you, others more obvious, even dramatic. Some will occur within days, others more gradually. One day you might realise that someone doesn't have the effect on you they once did. And the way you think, respond, act, feel, and the way you view your job, your family, and your life has changed for the better. Such is the magic of writing things down.

Affirmations

"Quite literally, the way you think shapes your life."

An affirmation is a helpful way of expressing a statement about yourself or an aspect of your life. And it's proven to be a fast, easy way to make a positive difference to your life. There are several ways you can use affirmations, such as thinking or saying them, yet w*riting* them down proves particularly powerful. Affirmations are more than simple feel good statements however, they are a way of programming yourself for success. That's because, quite literally, your thoughts shape your future.

Everything starts with an intention, a thought. If you want to get fitter, find a new home, increase your income or make new friends you first have a thought about it. Then you communicate this thought to yourself and/or others in the form of words and then go on to act on this. That's how all things come into being. This book started as a thought in Sallyann's mind, an intention to share with others how they could benefit from writing things down in a particular way. She communicated this to Mary and they started writing. And the final result is this book – an idea (thought) turned into a tangible physical form.

Affirmations are also an excellent way to help you alter any unhelpful self-limiting beliefs you may have about yourself or life in general. When beliefs are formed they become habits, so you may not have questioned how well a particular belief serves you – until now. Perhaps you have an unspoken belief about yourself that you'll never amount to much, for example. Yet remember: *a belief is not a truth.*

Imagine the difference between someone who believes that *life is limited* and someone who believes that *anything is possible*. Who is right? They both are. Because if you believe life is limited you will have limitation in your life. If you believe anything is possible you open yourself up to infinite possibilities.

The joy of using affirmations in your daily life is that you can use them anytime, anywhere. And when you can't write them down, you say them or think them. Throughout this chapter, you'll be given lots of examples of affirmations, including:

My environment is perfect

I love who I am and what I do

I have a solution to every challenge

My income increases constantly

You can also make up affirmations to suit your situation. The only thing you need to remember when doing this is to make them **Positive, Personal** and in the **Present**.

Make Them Positive:

Perhaps you've caught yourself thinking negatively or using negative language – an affirmation is a good way to get out of this habit. But you need to make the affirmation positive so instead of writing: *I don't want to use negative language* or *I no longer use negative language* write: *I use only positive language* or *I speak positively*. In the same way, if you regularly encounter someone who you feel drains you or vexes your spirit, instead of writing: *I don't want X in my life,* consider writing something along the following lines: *I always have loving people in my life* or *I am surrounded by people who nourish me.*

Make Them Personal:

In the main, it pays to make your affirmations personal to you. If you feel you want to be more aware of the choices you make in everyday life, you could write: *Everything in life is a choice* or *Choices abound in life*. These are effective, yet affirmations are more effective when you personalise them by writing: *I am always in choice; Choices abound in my life* or *I always make the best choices*. The difference is subtle, yet you can experiment for yourself with the following: Repeat *Life is full of choice* seven times. Now repeat *my life is full of choices* seven times. Which works best for you?

Make Them in the Present

Don't postpone your development by writing: *New opportunities will present themselves* or *I am going to change the way I work*. Talk as if what you want is already here by writing the affirmations in the present tense such as: *I am surrounded by opportunities* or *I love the way I work*.

The Power of Affirmations

One of the best things about affirmations is that you can use them to help you in *every* area of your life. They have the power to calm you, have you think more positively and to heal.

To help you get started we've selected ten areas of life that people experience challenges with and selected some affirmations for you. There will be a crossover between the areas, for instance: *Everything I experience reflects what's going on inside me* could be listed under every area so it makes sense to scan the affirmations listed under all the headings before you start. If the wording of one particular affirmation appeals to you more than another, use it or rephrase it to reflect your situation. *I am in harmony with my family* could be rewritten as *I am in harmony with all my colleagues* or *All my relationships are harmonious*.

As previously said, it is always preferable to state your affirmation as if what you want is already happening or already here. One of Sallyann's students however simply couldn't bring herself to write positive things about her body, so they compromised. She started by writing *I am willing to see myself differently.* Within a week her thinking had made a significant shift and she was able to write *I love all of my body.* So if you genuinely find yourself up against this sort of resistance write what we call a *willing* affirmation, such as: *I am willing to see my world differently; I am willing to see others differently; I am willing to let go of the past.* Simply expressing a willingness to let go can, almost magically, give you the ability to truly let go. And experience shows that if you have strong resistance with an affirmation, this is precisely the one you need to work on.

Health

Whether you want to improve your health or remain healthy, affirmations are an excellent healing tool. In addition you can use them to rid yourself of unhealthy habits, improve your perception of your body, achieve balance, release stress, help prevent illness and to instil healthier thought patterns.

I listen with love to my body's messages

I breathe in wellness

I heal myself on all levels

I am full of energy and vitality

I am well, I am healed

I eat and drink healthily

I love every part of me

I am calm and relaxed

I always treat my body with respect

Money

Whether you want to earn more, spend what you've got more wisely, or change your relationship with money, affirmations help. Your thoughts and beliefs affect what you earn, how you save and how generous you are with yourself and others. Consider the difference between people who believe that *money is always in short supply* to those who believe *there is always enough*. The former might consider they always have to be thrifty, make things last, save money just in case, and spend little on themselves, others and never on fun alone! The latter might trust that all they need will come to them, recognise that their income is more than just what they earn and share generously with others. Affirmations are a great way to start changing those self-limiting beliefs to ones that are more life-enhancing.

My income is unlimited

I enjoy a prosperous life

I live in abundance and there is plenty for everyone

I give and receive freely

Money is always plentiful

I am successful with money

New sources of income surround me

Career

When you spend a lot of time at work it makes sense to enjoy the time as much as possible. Even if you can't immediately change what you do and whom you do it with, you can change the way you view it. This is true if you work for yourself too, as your views on your business and your approach to clients have a direct impact on your success. Yet whether you work for yourself or for someone else, affirmations can dramatically improve your potential earnings, prospects, self-image and relationships with colleagues, clients and suppliers. They are also a great tool to help see you through periods of change, such as redundancy, job moves or retirement.

I speak positively

I always have choices

I create rewarding opportunities

I see my magnificence

I learn something new every day

I have an abundance of skills

I am motivated to serve

My potential is unlimited

I am always in the right place at the right time

I choose to enjoy my work

People need what I offer

My business is successful

Family and Friends

In addition to being a source of love and joy, families are often a source of unwanted pressure. The relationship between family members can be complex, put a strain on you and be a major stressor in your life. Your ability to deal effectively with these relationships will depend on many things, including how well you communicate together, how balanced your life is overall and the quality of other relationships, such as the ones you enjoy with friends.

Not all friendships are harmonious however, and occasionally you might need to reflect on the friends you've attracted into your life.

I allow myself to change my mind

I learn something new every day

I bless my family and friends with love

My heart is open to love and joy

All my relationships are harmonious

I am at peace with everyone

I am surrounded by people who love and appreciate me

I attract loving, caring people into my life

Spirituality

Sometimes life can be so busy that we drown out the blissful silence of our own soul or self. Whatever you call this infinite part of you, be it God, Buddha, Higher Self, Allah, The Creator, The Universe or whomever, in essence it isn't something that's separate from you, rather something of which you are a part. When you choose to reawaken your spiritual awareness you might find it difficult to know where to start. Our advice is to do something daily, whether it's to read uplifting quotes and books, meditate, pray or sit still silently and simply *be*. Repeated use of affirmations helps too.

I am at peace

I act with love, always

I trust that life is good

I am one with everything and everyone

Who I am makes a positive difference

I trust my inner knowing

The process of life supports me

I am love

My intuition guides me successfully

I serve the good of humankind

Who I am is unique and valuable

I am what God is doing

Significant Other

Rarely are our relationships with significant others free of challenges. Even the most loving relationships can falter. Fidelity, money, children, families, in-laws, sex, work, environment, and trust are just a few of the areas that cause friction. But maybe you're staying in a destructive relationship because on some level you think it's all you deserve or you fear being alone. Or maybe you feel love has passed you by. Whether you want to end a long-term relationship, rekindle an old one or reinvent the one you've got, affirmations help.

I listen with love

I make positive changes to my relationships

I am worthy of love

It is safe to love and be loved

It is safe to let love in and to give love

Life gives me what I ask for

I enjoy a beautiful loving relationship

I am the perfect partner

Home Environment

Does your home reflect you? Does it nurture you physically, spiritually and emotionally? If not, why not? What are you putting up with? Who are you stepping over? Maybe there's a good reason why at this moment your home is not how you want it to be, but has this become a habit? In your heart you know what you want and affirmations are an excellent place to start.

I live in harmony with my surroundings

I always live in beautiful places

My environment supports and nourishes me

My home is exactly how I want it to be

I am surrounded by things and people I enjoy

My home reflects the respect I have for myself

My home (office) reflects my beauty

My working (living) space is how I want it

Leisure and Fun

A balanced life is essential for wellness, so make space in your life for fun and leisure. If necessary, book appointments with yourself for this very purpose in the same way you do to visit doctors, clients, teachers and dentists. And fine yourself the way some dentists do if you fail to turn up!

If you were asked to teach somebody how to have fun, could you do it? Or have you forgotten what it's like to cry with laughter or laugh out loud? When did you last do something spontaneously silly or child-like (as opposed to childish!)? Can't remember? Read on. Fun is vital, life-enhancing and good for you, physically, emotionally and spiritually. And when you need to address the lack of fun and leisure in your life, affirmations are a great place to start...

I choose fun today

I am filled with fun and joy

I relax with life

I choose to make my life light

I laugh daily

I always have something to smile about

I am happy and joyful

Happiness is always with me

I have so much to smile about

Self Development

As you are reading this book, you are someone who has already made a decision to consciously increase your self-awareness and play a bigger part in creating your own future. Freeing yourself of the past is also a powerful way to move forward and take your life to a new level. Affirmations are an excellent self-development tool and will help you break self-defeating patterns and habits and introduce you to more nourishing ways of thinking and being.

I love myself totally

I forgive and let go with ease

I am perfect as I am

I love all

My beliefs bring treasures

I remember my magnificence

I love and approve of all of me

I express who I truly am

I am on a joyous journey

Whenever I need to learn, a teacher appears

All I need is revealed to me

How, When and Where to Write

The joy of writing affirmations is the flexibility you have over when, where and how you write. Sallyann's affirmation writing began many years ago:

"Each evening I would sit at the dining table with a lined writing pad and write the same affirmation over and over. And, as if to prove the power of this practice, I can still remember what I wrote – I love who I am and all that I do. I

told myself that I would write it a minimum of twenty times every night for a week. The truth was that once I got started I didn't want to stop. Seeing these words come from me onto the page was empowering and I would often write it out a hundred or more times every night."

Many people write the same affirmation over and over for a week or two, sometimes more, particularly if they're working on a specific aspect of themselves or their lives. Others write a different affirmation every day, rotating their favourite ones. The act of writing it down is what counts, not when, how and where you choose to do this. Many people write their affirmations first thing in the morning, others at the end of the day. Whenever you choose you'll discover the affirmation's power once you've committed it to paper as it becomes a recurring thought that stays with you.

The effective part is that you write the affirmation repeatedly, a minimum of ten times. And on the occasions you can't write them down, recite them mentally. In fact, we suggest you do this anyway to help reinforce what you write.

A lined legal or spiral bound pad is useful for writing affirmations and a pen that allows you to write fluidly across the page. And remember, the following are guidelines, not rules!

- choose your affirmation

- sit somewhere comfortable with your pad and pen

- write the affirmation across the page, repeating it mentally as you write

- write it a minimum of ten times daily (more if you wish and time allows)

Because affirmations are short, you can write them down at any opportunity throughout the day to help reinforce them – on a napkin when you're having a coffee, on a train or flight, or sat in a waiting room.

Tips:

- use the same affirmation for a week or more (to work on a particular challenge)

- try different coloured pens and papers

- write affirmations on post-it notes and stick up in a prominent place such as on your bathroom mirror, fridge, doors, computer, dashboard or inside your wallet.

- use affirmations which work for you, trust your intuition on this

Make It Fun!

Be creative and make your own affirmation cards. Cut coloured card into business or index sized cards. Write your chosen affirmation on the card using felt or calligraphy pens (or generate it on a computer) and decorate around it as you wish. You could keep this in your purse or wallet, or in a frame or cardholder on your desk or bedside table.

True Life Stories...

There are countless examples of how people have transformed negative situations and beliefs about themselves with the help of this technique. Here's one:

I was going through a low period in my life. The children had left home, my partner seemed remote and I felt everybody else had a life except me. I began writing affirmations at a friend's suggestion, though if I'm honest, I didn't think it could work. Too simple. I started off with I always speak and think positively. *I remember laughing to myself as I first wrote it down; it seemed so ironic. Yet I wrote it numerous times morning and night. Within a week I can honestly say I felt different, more positive about myself than I'd done in a long time. I found myself remembering it every time I was about to say something negative about me and my life and would either stay quiet or say something positive. Looking back I can see it was a turning point – Geraldine*

Finally...

As with other ways of writing suggested in this book, writing affirmations isn't something you do only when you face a particular challenge. They are a great way of maintaining a positive enthusiastic approach to yourself and life. And for something so seemingly simple the rewards are life-changing, because in truth they are much more. If you use the affirmation *I live in abundance* for example, you effectively acknowledge all the good in your life – family, friends, car, home, money, health, food, the freedom to vote, worship, express opinions and more. Yes, affirmations are far more than they initially seem. They are a way of moving from negativity, mistrust and fear to a place of confidence, trust and gratitude. To a place of contentment and love where you know that all is well in your world.

Life Changing Lists

"It was there on the list in front of me.
And I wouldn't have believed it if I hadn't written it myself.
But I knew it was truth."

List writing is an excellent way of bringing something to your full attention. Seeing the information there on the paper in front of you, in black and white so to speak, singles it out from all the other mental clutter whizzing around in your head. Certainly the information carries more impact. And you won't find a single *To Do* or *Not to Do* list here, as this is list writing with a difference. Their only requirement is that, as with all the writing activities suggested in this book, you are completely honest.

The lists suggested in this chapter encourage you to become more self-aware, to look at your life and your way of being in greater detail. You gain an appreciation of who you are and what you have. And you get to finally admit to who and what you've been stepping around.

What you do with all this information is up to you. Many of you will find it liberating to acknowledge your true situation in this way, even if you choose to do nothing about it for the time being. At least you've chosen honesty and revealed your true self to yourself, maybe for the first time (as opposed to being who you think others want you to be). In this sense writing lists is something you might choose to do before moving on to writing affirmations, letters or journaling, for example, as the latter all help bring about the changes you desire.

The Living in Gratitude List

It is all too easy to overlook the things that work in our lives. The days when the sun shines, or we get that much needed rain; the days our family are healthy and our work fulfilling; the days we look fantastic in that outfit, have a job, can pay the rent, have a bed to sleep in and the car starts and the bus arrives on time.

You get the idea. It's only when those things start to go awry that we notice. That's why a gratitude list is so powerful. It helps you:

- be more appreciative of what you have *while you have it*

- be more aware of all the things you might take for granted daily – fresh running water, roads, delivery people, for example

- be more aware of our interconnection and need of each other

- remove blocks to attracting abundance into your life

- focus on all that you have (as opposed to what you lack)

- turn negative emotions such as fear to more life-enhancing ones of joy and love

- realise a brighter future

When, How and Where to Write

Last thing at night or first thing in the morning are the preferred times to write this list. Yet you will experience great benefits by writing it at any time of the day. Write a fresh list daily and commit to doing it *every* day for at least a month. This gets you into the habit of appreciating, and developing that all essential attitude of gratitude.

Write out at least seven things for which you are grateful. And if you really don't feel as if you have anything to be grateful for, start with the air that you breathe, your eyesight (if you have eyesight), the roof over your head or your children or pets. There is *always* something and someone to be grateful for. If you sit watching television feeling fed up with the world, you can only do so because people have worked to make the programmes. And still you couldn't watch it without those who work at generating the electricity that powers your set, or the people who made the set, so be grateful for these people at least.

One of Sallyann's clients told her: *One day I decided to make a list of all the things that I felt were right with me and my life; all the things I could be grateful for. The list was far longer than I thought! It was a positive experience and now I make a gratitude list daily.*

Many people write more than fifty things daily and it's true that when you focus your mind on gratitude this way you will find more and more to appreciate.

You can write this list on anything, yet we suggest you treat yourself to a book that appeals to you. Whether it's lined or unlined pages, loose or bound pages, covered in pictures of flowers, cars or horses, let it reflect your taste. Sallyann buys lined writing books, which she labels *Gratitudes*. She writes in it last thing at night, usually, and says it's amazing what spills forth.

I am Grateful For...

The following are examples from a variety of people's gratitude lists who are willing for us to share them with you:

The African violet on the windowsill flowered today

The blood donor whose blood I received – God bless you

The wine stain came off the new carpet

My comfy bed

Barry and the kids

My new wheelchair

This frothy hot coffee

Living another day

Mum's funeral being so well attended

My computer not crashing as it has done every other day this week!

The gift of peace this afternoon

My business being in profit

I voted!

Showing gratitude in this way really does work. And as the above selection shows, the appreciation can be for something as big as being alive to seemingly smaller pleasures such as a cup of frothy coffee. Don't wait until you lose something or someone to make a habit of appreciation, for it's often only then we realise *there are no small pleasures in life.*

When Graham's wife died he treasured his memories and photos of the great travels they went on together to India and other far-flung destinations, and the fun-filled Christmas and Easter holidays they always shared with their families. But it was the small things he missed. Watching her draw back the bedroom curtains first thing in the morning and seeing her laugh as he moaned about the daylight. The cups of tea they shared in quiet when they both sat reading. *'I never even considered those things at the time,'* he says. *'Yet now they stand out as some of the things I miss most about her.'*

Be grateful for all you have right now, today, this minute. Be appreciative and enjoy, and in doing so you open yourself up to a remarkable flow of abundance.

The Uplifting/Draining List

There are things and people in your life who add positively to your energy. You feel energised or uplifted when you're surrounded by these people or doing these things. So much so that you sometimes lose track of time or sense of place. In much the same way there are people and things that deplete or lower your energy and leave you feeling drained and lethargic.

You probably come across people and situations daily which fit into one of these categories – energising or draining. And listing these helps you:

- be aware of what and who you are stepping around

- become fully aware of what and who you want more of

- become fully aware of what and who you want less of

- prioritise and act in a way that brings about positive change

When, How and Where to Write

It doesn't matter what time of day you choose to do this list. It's far more important that you choose a time when you won't be interrupted. Relax somewhere comfortable and allow yourself at least thirty minutes to make the initial list. Once you've made the list, you need time to ask yourself certain questions and reflect on the answers, so allow another hour for this. Some people find it beneficial to write the list and return to it later or the following day for the reflective part. Others find that splitting it this way interrupts their contemplative mood. All we ask is that you don't rush the second part of this exercise. Come back to it when you have more time. You are worth this.

Divide a large sheet of paper into two columns by drawing a line down the centre of the page. In the left hand column you write what uplifts or energises you. And in the right hand column you list what drains or depletes your energy. Take your time, be specific and be absolutely honest as this list is for your eyes only.

The following is an example:

Energises Me:	*Drains Me:*
Walking in nature, forests etc.	*Negative people, such as Lydia*
Inspiring stories	*Gossip and trivia, with the 'coffee set'*
People who make the best of things	*Self-pitying people (Marge, Bill)*
Writing funny verses	*Food shopping with kids in tow*
Decorating	*Arguing*
Being with good friends, Gail etc	*Watching too much television*
Pottering in Garden	*Opinionated people (Clive, Sandy)*
Having a good laugh	*Working with moaners (Bill, Gilly)*
Being acknowledged	*Untidy home*
Meditation	*Mental clutter*
Reaching work targets	*Friends who ask me to do things they know I don't want to do*
Pampering myself	*Being overdrawn so heavily*
Eating healthily	*Being indecisive*

If you find it difficult to come up with things to list, mentally working your way through an average week might help. Be aware of where you get sensations in your body – usually these are in your stomach and heart areas – and see what this tells you. Do you get a sinking or sickly feeling in your stomach when you think of work as it's something that drains you? Or do you get a smile on your face or an exhilarated feeling in your body as it's something that energises you? Or think back to times you've enjoyed and times you haven't, what was in place at those times? Who were present? What were you doing? Use these answers to feed your list and make the lists as long as they need to be.

If specific people energise or drain you write their names on your list. You may feel uncomfortable about doing this, yet it's the reluctance to see written before you what you're carrying in your heart that makes it wise. After all, this list is for your eyes only. And you did agree to be honest.

Next Step...

Firstly, sit back and congratulate yourself. Spending time on you in this way is important. The point of this list is that you now have before you a list of people and situations that energise you and a list of people and situations that drain you. If you still have an hour, or more, free of interruptions, continue with the next step. If not, please wait until you have.

This is your opportunity to reflect on what you've written. Slowly work your way down the list of what energises you. Look at each item in turn and ask yourself when did you last do this activity or see this person? How much of your life is filled with what energises you? Fifty per cent? Less? More?

Now do the same with the list that drains you. How much of your life is filled with people and situations that drain you?

The idea of the list is to bring into focus what you're putting up with and who or what you're stepping around. The information is plain and clear and it's there in front of you and there are two more questions to ask.

The first question is *why*?

Why, when you enjoy writing funny verses do you only do it twice a year? Why drink coffee with the coffee-set when it drains you? Why haven't you connected with friends for such a long time when it means so much to you? Why spend so much time with Lydia when her negativity drains you? There will be as many answers as ways of asking the question and honesty is the key. Don't say you feel obliged to spend time with Lydia because you've known her for so long and she can't help being the way she is. Be honest. Maybe you enjoy being negative too. Maybe listening to her moan about her life makes you feel better about yours. Maybe you feel awkward around confident, positive people. Worse still, perhaps you don't know any. Why? Perhaps because you're more negative than you thought and positive people avoid you!

The key with the *why* question is to whittle your answers down to the truth. *The whole truth and nothing but the truth.*

The next question is: What choices do I make now?

This is the most important question because now you're focusing on the solution, not the problem! And the answer to this is unique to you and your situation. One thing is for sure, if you do nothing different, nothing will change. It may be that you want to live with this new found knowledge for a while. Go about your daily business and stand back, metaphorically, to witness your way of being in the world. To be aware of the part you've played in your life being this way. Yet don't allow reflection to become a substitute for doing nothing. The answer will start with something as simple as thinking a new way. Indeed, that's how everything starts!

True Life Example

Gilly decided that the next time she met Lydia she wouldn't engage in negative talk. Every time Lydia moaned about something, Gilly said,' Yeah, but…' and counteracted it with something more positive. Eventually Lydia said, 'You seem happy today, have you won the lottery or something?' Gilly decided to be open. 'No,' she answered. 'I just got to realising how negative my talk can be at times, so I'm choosing to view everything more positively. I'd hate to get a reputation for being miserable and negative.' Lydia smiled. 'Yeah, y'know I've noticed myself doing the same. Perhaps we can keep a check on each other!' Gilly says that her relationship with Lydia has now altered beyond recognition. She looks forward to their meetings so much so that they meet more often now.

Many of your answers will be down to the way you view and value yourself, and many more about prioritising. There are only 24 hours in everyone's day and by saying yes to an hour with the coffee-set you are saying no to an hour's painting, writing, walking, having a long hot soak in the bath or being with good friends. **Repeat: By saying *yes* to something or someone you are saying no to something else.** *Always.*

Identify the true reasons behind your challenge, work on one area at a time and give it your best shot. And remember, the other chapters in this book will help you. And don't stop making lists. Repeat the exercise every so often. Here's to you and the magic of writing things down!

Dream Discoveries

"Dreams are the touchstones of our characters."

(Henry David Thoreau)

Psychologists suggest that most of our dreams are about immediate concerns in our lives. Some dreams can help you understand yourself and what motivates you, and others could be a trial run for dealing with waking daytime challenges. Dreams are the language of the unconscious and many people believe they are a way for your higher self to communicate with you. And the unfolding of a dream allows you to deal with issues as and when you are ready.

Dreaming occurs during a period of sleep called Rapid Eye Movement (REM) and some scientists believe this happens so you can exercise your brain. In a waking state, messages are constantly circulating through your brain cells allowing you to think, move, digest information and make sense of your surroundings and what is happening in your life. When you sleep, dreams exercise the channels between the billions of brain cells in your head, keeping you fresh and alert. During REM sleep your muscles become inert and this is the reason many people dream that they are trying to run away from something only to find their legs heavy and unable to move.

The idea that dreams are brain exercises is given credibility by the fact that you have the greatest amount of REM sleep in your formative years when there is much learning to be done. Brain Waves or electrical patterns measuring brain activity look much the same during REM sleep and when we are fully awake, but a different pattern emerges during other types of sleep.

Dream Types

- *Bad Dreams or Nightmares.* These can be influenced by several factors including watching scary movies. The dream serves the function of processing emotionally charged events that you witnessed but did not necessarily experience, such as the scary movie scenario. It is considered important to unburden your emotions by processing and dealing with the scenes witnessed

- *Dreams as Psyche Cleansers.* The mind processes information on many levels and, as with a computer, if you put trash into your computer-like subconscious you get trash out. Dreams cleanse the mind, ridding it of the garbage so it no longer pollutes itself. The best way to purge these dreams is to avoid the garbage!

- *Dreams as messages.* Dreams can be messages from your subconscious telling you that you are not being true to yourself or that you're not living according to your values or rules. They can also reveal that your behaviour is causing harm to yourself or others and alert you to an imbalance between the needs of your ego and the needs of your higher self

- *Dreams as Revelations.* These types of dreams occur on a super-conscious level and lead to discoveries and insights particularly in science and create inspiration in art. Robert Louis Stevenson claimed that the idea for his famous book of the split personality, Dr Jekyll and Mr Hyde, originated in a dream. On this level, you are able to make contact with your higher self and probe another level of consciousness

- *The Symbolism of Dreams.* You need to develop a deeper understanding of the symbolic language of the dream state in order to understand yourself better. Symbolism plays an important part in this process and your mind's computer sometimes filters out unpleasant incidents to tone down threatening imagery. The issue at stake then appears in a more agreeable light so the overall picture is less disturbing. We need to be aware of this when we interpret our dreams. There are three main types of symbolism.

(1) **Personal** – for example, a St Christopher medallion on a chain might symbolise protection while travelling to one person, but if you caught yours in the car door and nearly strangled yourself you might feel differently.

(2) **Cultural** – for example the swan signifies purity and grace in some cultures but a prophecy of death in others.

(3) **Universal** – that are common to all cultures, such as the mother and father figures.

Why Keep a Dream Diary?

You can live a more enriched life by working with the energy and insight of your dreams. Dreams offer you a pathway to creativity, healing and understanding. Research suggests that it's possible to dream your way to a better life and by changing the way you dream, take control of your destiny. Dreams can also provide solutions to daily problems. If anything is troubling writing teacher, Jan Valpy, she writes it down on a peace of paper and slips it under her pillow before retiring for the night. A response or a solution will come to her in a dream and when she wakes she has her answer.

Recording your dreams helps you clarify and understand their messages, sometimes showing a pattern that can be an indication of matters that need your attention. This information can be used to help you make better life choices and show you how to help others with their life challenges. Dreaming gives you access to another level of consciousness and allows you to communicate successfully with your higher self. Dreams can also help you maintain equilibrium by showing you dangers and presenting you with opportunities that you would not be aware of in your waking moments.

How to Record Your Dreams

A dream diary is similar to a daily diary but you record your sleeping adventures instead of your waking ones. Keep paper and pen beside your bedside table so you can write down your dreams on waking otherwise they tend to be forgotten especially when your daily life starts making demands. The more detail you recall the better even if it doesn't make sense because you may discover its importance when you come to interpret your dreams.

Avoid having an immediate theory about what your dreams may mean as this can lead you to ignore things which you assume to be irrelevant but turn out, given time, to be important. If you can't recall the dream, write down the feelings or emotions you had on waking. With regular practice you will be able to remember your dreams and record them. And whilst you might now consider waking up to record your dreams a chore, it soon becomes an exciting prospect!

Tips:

- put pen to paper as soon as you wake as dreams fade rapidly

- write the day (Friday, Monday) and full date at the top of a sheet of blank paper before retiring every night. This can help you reveal sequences or series of dreams. Number the dreams too as some nights you may wake to record something more than once and you need to record the order of dreaming (together with times, if possible)

- write down the events of your dream in the order in which they appear. This may seem unimportant especially if the events don't appear to be related. When interpreting dreams later on, the relationship between incidents often becomes clear

- make a note of the people who were in the dream. What did they say and do? If they seemed familiar to you, but you weren't sure who they were, see if you can think of someone in your waking life they closely resemble. Be as detailed as possible, however trivial your observations may seem

- if you really can't recall your dream now you're awake, record how you feel

- if there is a familiar scene in your dream record the differences between the dream place and how the scene appears in waking life. For instance in a room, is the dream furniture the same style and colour and in the same place as in the waking situation?

- record any differences between well-known people in the dream and people in your daily environment. Are they the same age? Do they have the same hairstyle or hair colour? Are they wearing the same style of clothes?

- make a note of any characters that may be symbolic, animals, for instance, spectres or objects that took on human characteristics in the dream

- keep a track of recurring events, themes or characters. Do they always occur or behave in the same way in repeated dreams? If not, record the differences

- make a note of all the colours you experience. People often say they dream in black and white because colour fades faster than other aspects of a dream

- write down your reaction to the events that occurred in your dream, not just on a physical level but your emotional response to what happened. Write down how you feel now that the dream is over

- don't rely on your memory. Write down everything you remember even if you think it's not important, it may prove to have a connection with another incident on another occasion

True Life Example

Once you've collected all the information on paper, you'll want to record it in your dream diary. Here's an example of two consecutive entries in a friend's dream diary:

17 November 2000

Dream 22

Timed: before 3 a.m.

Dreamt I was watching Billy stalk a hare beside a high perimeter fence. The fence was metal chicken-wire material and leaning over at the top. The ground was hard bare compacted brown earth except for some long green blades of grass where the hare sat. The hare was two-colour beige and russet! I watched Billy until I realised he would make a go for the hare unless I stopped him. There was a gap under the fence the hare could fit through, but it didn't seem to notice. It didn't even seem to recognise it was in danger. It was broad daylight and I got the feeling I was on the edge of an airfield. I told Graham that Billy was stalking as Graham was with me then (I was suddenly aware he was behind me). I knew he was there, but didn't turn to see him.

    Atmosphere: normal at first, then sensed urgency
    Mood: Soft, at first, slowly getting tense
    Signs and Symbols: Hare
    Previous association: Billy (the cat) stalking

17 November 2000

Dream 23

Timed: before 7 a.m.

Dreamt I was driving around a seaside town (it was supposed to be Minehead though it was on the north-east coast of England – somewhere I haven't visited) on a series of toy-like flyovers. It was as if I was driving through a virtual toy-town with large blue and grey buildings and mostly unoccupied roads. I was on my own in the car.

Atmosphere: safe
Mood: Lonely
Signs and Symbols: crossover of roads. Buildings
Previous association: have dreamt this and this location before

Interpreting Your Dreams

Many articles and books have been written about the meanings of dreams but the best person to interpret your dreams is <u>you</u>. As mentioned before, symbolism is a prominent feature when trying to make sense of dreams. But symbolism can mean different things to different people and different cultures. It's too easy to seek a solution in a book of ready-made answers instead of trying to figure out the reason for the dream yourself and the message or guidance it is giving.

We guess nobody would choose to have nightmares, but nightmares are just unfinished dreams. You encounter something so frightening or disturbing in your sleep that you deliberately wake up and feel thankful that it *was only a dream*. Nightmares guide you however just as much as ordinary dreams. Maybe you have ignored the messages of these ordinary dreams or even the messages of waking life. Forced to try another tactic, your higher self has this dream become so loud that your sleep is disturbed resulting in a nightmare.

True Life Dreams

Mary once had a nightmare that she was walking alone late at night down a dark alleyway. A sinister looking man stepped into her path and refused to let her pass. She woke up before his behaviour became too threatening. She remembers saying to herself in the dream, 'Now you've done it, you've taken a risk with your security once too often and you're going to pay the price.' She said it was such a relief to wake up and she understood the nightmare was giving her a message about her habit of walking home alone from town late at night.

Following the dream, Mary resolved to take her car when she was out on dark evenings, being sure to park in a well lit, busy area. She bought a cell phone and obtained comprehensive breakdown cover for the car. Things that she had been meaning to do for a while but kept putting off. The nightmare made her realise how important safety and security was for her to fully enjoy her active social life.

You can get over your nightmare fears by turning around and confronting the issues in a determined fashion and by asking the threat, *'Who are you? Why are you pursuing me? What do you have to tell me?'* Trying to get back inside the dream, however scary, and dreaming on to a resolution or closure can sometimes help. Once you understand that there is a message there somewhere and the dream is not just an exercise in terror, you can be calm, strong and face the situation head-on.

Before you try to analyse your dream, listen to what your body and your feelings tell you. Trust your intuition as it indicates what is going on. The message may be positive or negative, and may relate to a real situation. Think of a dream as being like a poem where there is often another level of meaning as well as the dictionary definition of the words. As poetry catches the vibrations of sound and rhythm, so dreams capture the resonance of image. It's difficult to tell the story of a poem and do it justice, equally it's difficult to recount a dream using words. Words don't always capture the mood, feeling or sentiment in which case you describe the experience as best you can. Referring back to your notes a few times at a later stage will often give you a greater insight and enable you to improve the language.

Often dream messages are about the future but you misinterpret them because:

- you make mistakes identifying people and places

- you are unable to determine how far in the future the dreamed of event might be

- you mistake a real event for a symbolic one or vice-versa

- you don't see the whole picture of the future event which restricts your interpretation

- you confuse experiences because you dream on different levels

Only *you* can know the true meaning of your dreams. The difficulty arises because there are often several ways you can interpret your dream. For instance, an untidy office may feature in your dream. You then go to work and find a complete mess because someone has accidentally turned on the fan by your desk and scattered paperwork far and wide. Now the dream could have just been predicting the event or it could signify that your working life is in disarray and you need to prioritize the various aspects of your job, your motivation and commitment.

Dreaming of a natural disaster may symbolize a coming crisis in your life though it can be an accurate prediction of a forthcoming event. Sallyann experienced a vivid dream about an incident in the UK when she was staying in India. She woke, heart thumping and noted the time on the clock. The next day she discovered the incident happened for real in the UK at precisely the same time she dreamt about it all those thousands of miles away.

Creative Ways to Further Explore Your Dreams

Here are some suggestions for further exploratory work on dreams:

1. Give your dream a title and identify a genre such as romance, melodrama, science fiction

2. Explore the main character and the use of the five senses

3. Write the main character's mini biography

4. Imagine the characters are on stage and use dialogue as in a play

5. Write the story in a few succinct paragraphs as you would for a book cover to entice readers to buy your novel

6. Imagine the dream story is an outside broadcast and you are a commentator

7. Imagine you are interviewing the main character

8. Write the next chapter of the story

9. Explore who you were in the dream

10. Finally, explore the person or aspect of the dream that puzzles you

These exercises will help you write freely and intuitively and this is where the healing and the emotional unburdening can assist you to address issues and forge the link between waking and dreaming. A good idea is to share your dreams with a friend, using the friend not as an interpreter but as a facilitator or helper. You can discuss your dreams and bounce ideas off each other, remembering to always allow the dreamer to find *their own* meaning to the dream.

You need to be disciplined to be a successful dream journalist, yet it is truly worthwhile. The results can often give you a fascinating and meaningful insight into you and your life.

Poetic Licence

"Poetry is the spontaneous overflow of powerful feelings: it takes its origin from emotion collected in tranquillity."

(William Wordsworth)

Poetry is a piece of imaginative writing in verse form. Writing which allows you to express your feelings or to describe a place or event. And this imaginative way of expressing yourself helps you make sense of your life. Poetry is rife with metaphor (*Jane felt blue* – blue was the metaphor) and the use of metaphor is a powerful element. Crafting words into a poetic form increases their impact on you the writer, and you the reader. And by creating order out of mental muddle and clutter you release strong emotions, which is why writing poetry is so therapeutic.

When you want to deal with issues that cause you concern or block you, poetry has a healing value. That's because when you write freely and intuitively you encapsulate experiences, thoughts, feelings and ideas in a succinct way. You gain a clear-sightedness and reveal another level of meaning often not available to your conscious mind.

People sigh when they're asked to write a poem, assuming it has to be deeply meaningful and start to say things such as '*I can't...*' or '*I'm no good at poetry.*' So, at workshops, Mary often asks people to write their name down the edge of the page and to start each line of their poem with the next letter of their name, as follows (Oh, and they only have three minutes to complete this!) – Sallyann wrote the following:

She looked at the class

And smiled

Let's not get hung up on this

Let's not protest

Yawning was heard

As she set the timer!

Now you're three minutes is up

Neville, that's simply brilliant!

Everyone at the sessions writes a poem in three minutes. And it's precisely because they have so little time that they are willing to let go and write whatever comes into their head. The results are often poignant, revealing and side-splittingly funny. And we always end up doing more forms of quick poetry. Try it!

The Rhythm of Life

When you wax lyrical the rhythm alone can be healing. Were you asked to repeat multiplication tables at school?

Once two is two
Two twos are four
Three twos are six
Four twos are eight
Five twos are ten
          and so on…

There is something comforting in that repetitive rhythm, of chanting to a regular beat. At school did you have to memorise pages and pages of poetry and recite it out loud as a class? When you talk to older people it's surprising how many of them know by heart poems such as *Tennyson's* 'The Lady of Shallott' which contained 19 verses of 9 lines and began:

On either side the river lie
Long fields of barley and of rye
That clothes the world and meet the sky
And thro' the field the road runs by
To many tower'd Camelot.

Another one of Mary's classroom favourites was *Kubla Khan* by Samuel Taylor Coleridge. She recalls this poem being chosen often during the Friday afternoon free period at her school when it was up to the students to decide on the activity. It was the rhythm that captivated her and her classmates, as they didn't understand all the words they were repeating and to this day Mary says she still doesn't know what *athwart a cedarn cover* means.

Music, which plays a vital role in many people's lives, can be compared to poetry with its elements of rhythm and pitch. Rhythm, the strong regular repeated pattern in music, equates to the measured flow of words or phrases in verse or prose and pitch in music is likened to tone in writing. In this way, writing to a musical formula (a song) can be most enjoyable.

Before You Write

Remember that as with any creative style, poetry is subjective and its beauty is in the ear of the listener. What one person thinks of as brilliant, another will consign to the waste bin! There is a poem which consists of lists of single words on the outer edges of facing pages. As you read, you mimic watching a tennis match. Clever, but is that poetry? Some people think so, others say not.

The point to make here is that creating words on paper by expressing yourself freely and intuitively releases pent up emotion and aids the healing process. It helps you express joy and sadness, resentment and gratitude. It frees you up mentally and emotionally by getting it out from within – whatever your particular *it* is. You don't have to compose a masterpiece (what is a masterpiece anyway?) and remember, nobody has to read this. Spelling and grammar are not important, you just have to truly express your feelings as succinctly as possible. Then you get to experience the magic of writing things down.

Tips:

The more short, sharp words you use, the more tension you create. This gives a feeling of energy and puts action into your writing. Use this style when you want your verse to feel more urgent and exciting.

Cats pounce
Mice quiver
Claws trounce
Death's shiver

On the other hand, when you want to create a relaxing or refined ambience, use multi-syllable words as they generate a feeling of calm and can also sound sophisticated. It is the length of the words and not the number in one line that's important so don't be tempted to waste words.

Water lilies slumbering
Concealing corpulent creatures
Denizens of darkness
No lightness of being

In reply to the question 'How can you become a poet?' *Eve Merriam* says:

take the leaf of a tree

trace its exact shape
the outside edges
and inner lines
memorise the way it is fastened to the twig
(and how the twig arches from the branch)

how it springs forth in April
how it is panoplied in August
crumple it in your hand
so that you smell its end-of-summer sadness
chew its woody stem
listen to its autumn rattle
watch as it atomizes in the November air
then in winter
where there is no leaf left
    INVENT ONE

What to Write or Invent

Someone once said that writing poetry is 10% inspiration and 90% perspiration, yet it doesn't have to be as difficult as it sounds. Remember this book gives you guidelines not rules! One way to get started is to take a newspaper or magazine and find a story or an article that catches your eye. As you read, highlight or underline any words that speak to you or jump out at you from the page. Write these words down in lines of roughly equal length. You'll be surprised at the impact they can have and you can use them as a basis or guide to carry on or expand the poem.

A student of Mary's completed this exercise using a newspaper article about the Middle East. The words she chose were: *desert; sun; shadow; protection; shade; sighs; hands; sore; watch; face; progress* and *make haste*. Although she could have grouped these words together in twos or threes per line, she decided to write a poem that included one of her chosen words in each line as follows:

*Alone in the **desert***
*Burned up by the **sun***
*A **shadow** approaches*
*Protection is **spun***
*Affording **shade***
*From the zephyr's **sighs***

***Hands** slowly fall*
*Away from **sore** eyes*
*To **watch** gentle teasing*
*On an undefined **face***
*The way to make **progress***
*Is not to **make haste***

The student gradually realized that she was writing about a current relationship. She felt that she and her boyfriend were getting involved too quickly and this was making her feel uneasy. She went on to write two more verses that revealed a strategy for dealing with this situation.

A good way to learn about poetry is to read it, much and often. And if you do that, you can follow this idea about writing poetry quickly and easily. Chose a poem that you enjoy reading and change the words. Remember to keep the same rhythm going and it will flow in the same way as the original. Mary created the following in a writing class when she was concerned about her weight. It's based on Lord Byron's poem *She walks in beauty like the night.*

She picks the chocolates, brown and white
The cloying limes are such a prize
And all that's best of dark and light
Is manifested in her size
Thus blocking out a day that's bright
With gaudy tents that are outsize!

Tips:

- remember rhythm – it's said a poem isn't complete until all the lines scan or form a balanced pattern

- last words on lines of poems do not have to rhyme – free verse is allowed!

- remove all unnecessary words and keep the text tight

- use imagery, the senses and metaphor

- read more poetry and read it out loud to get a feeling for rhythm

- as with any form of writing, the more you write the easier it gets!

More Poetry Ideas

If all this sounds too complicated and technical, let's go back to basics and write a simple name poem. This is a good way to focus on the influence people around you have on your life. Just follow the 10 steps:

Line 1   your first name
Line 2   'it means' and then 3 adjectives that describe you
Line 3   'it is the number' then any number you choose
Line 4   'it is like' describe a colour but don't name it
Line 5   'it is' describe a happy experience
Line 6   'it is the memory' name someone who has been significant in your life
Line 7   'who taught me' name 2 values
Line 8   'when he/she' describe how they displayed the qualities in line 7
Line 9   'my name is' your first name
Line 10   'it means' write 1 or 2 sentences about something important you believe about life

Example:

Jenny
It means strong, compassionate, honest
It is a million
It is like summer sunshine
It is swimming in shallow rock pools
It is the memory of a kind father
Who taught me patience and trust

When he took me fishing
My name is Jenny
It means everything comes to she who waits

If composing a poem to the above format fails to give you an idea for further writing, try writing a three verse 'I am' poem which gets you to focus on your own characteristics. There should be something here that you can pull out and elaborate on in your own way. Watch for lines that speak to you or seem to have more significance than others. Then use one of these lines as the title of your poem.

I am	(two special characteristics)
I wonder	(something you are curious about)
I hear	(an imaginary sound)
I see	(an imaginary sight)
I want	(an actual desire)
I am	(repeat first line of poem)
I pretend	(something you pretend to do)
I feel	(a feeling about something imaginary)
I touch	(an imaginary touch)
I worry	(something that really bothers you)
I cry	(something that makes you sad)
I am	(repeat first line of poem)
I understand	(something you know is true)
I say	(something you believe in)
I dream	(something you dream about)
I try	(something you make an effort for)
I hope	(something you hope for)
I am	(repeat first line of poem)

An Example:

I Touch God

I am creative and talented
I wonder about the world

I hear sounds of nature
I see birds in flight
I want peace and harmony
I am creative and talented.

I pretend to be brave
I feel unsure
I touch God
I worry about the future
I cry about neglect
I am creative and talented.

I understand I am not alone
I say I am learning
I dream of fulfilment
I try my best
I hope I achieve it
I am creative and talented.

Being economical with words is the key to writing poetically. And having to be as brief as possible makes you think about *exactly* what you want to say and nothing else. This can be helpful when trying to sort out emotions and issues. If this seems difficult, express what you're feeling in as many words as you want and then try and pare them down to the bare bones so you are left with your poem. Japanese haiku, poems of 17 syllables usually in 5-7-5 formations can be useful here as they are short and simple to write. Here is an example:

Since-you-went-a-way   (5 syllables)
Life-is-hard-to-con-sid-er (7 syllables)
Each-and-ev-ery-day   (5 syllables)

They don't have to rhyme but they do need to tell the story, feeling or idea in only three lines. Here's another:

The blind musician
Extending an old tin cup
Collects a snowflake

Try writing a haiku or a conventional poem, if you prefer, about something that interests you such as your cat or your dog, your garden or the sunset. Think about what makes it special. Does your dog have long ears that look like old socks? Does your sun sink over water, the mountains or the industrial estate? Pay attention to the little things, the details that make your dog or the sunset different from anything else. Don't write that your garden is nice or the sunset pretty. Instead write specifically about those things that make your garden nice and the sunset pretty. When you write this way you make a picture out of words.

Finally

Read your poem aloud. Does it help you understand what you are trying to convey? Do you like the way your words sound together? Is there feeling expressed in your poem? If so, what feelings – joy, sorrow, anger, resentment, fun, love, perhaps? Will somebody else reading your words feel what you felt? Read what you've written several times and don't be afraid to change the words. Make sure your work says exactly what you want it to say. Then again, you don't have to revisit anything you write – the magic happens when you write it down!

Your Story

"I think I could have written a secret book and kept it in a drawer somewhere and still have been happier."

Nigel Slater

When you think about writing the story of your life, your mind invariably goes back to your first memory, which, for most of us, lives back in our childhood. This is a good place to start, at the beginning as it were. On the first page of his autobiographical novel, *Angela's Ashes,* Frank McCourt wrote:

When I look back on my childhood, I wonder how I survived at all. It was of course a miserable childhood; the happy childhood is hardly worth your while…'

Stories published about people's childhoods are rarely happy ones, especially if the author isn't famous. It's rare even if they are famous; consider Pamela Stephenson's biography of Scottish comedian Billy Connolly. Occasionally there is an uncommon find such as Andrew Moellar's biography of happy chappy Chris Spencer, but this is only available on the internet at the time of writing. It seems that most people who choose to write their story are those whose childhood experiences were at best unpleasant, at worst, traumatic or life-threatening. Why? The act of writing is therapeutic. The relief at letting out that what has been locked inside for so long unburdens you. You have spoken, albeit on the page in words, and you gain a fresh perspective on events, people and your life. And ultimately grow in self-worth.

Nigel Slater, chef and author of *Toast*, admits part of his childhood was so unhappy that he wanted to blot it out. Now he says that writing the book provided a therapy all of its own.

'Now I feel a lot better just for writing it down. I am not sure I actually needed to publish it. I think I could have written a secret book and kept it in a drawer somewhere and still have been happier.'

Even if your childhood was happy you may have concerns going back to your formative years, which have led you to hold self-limiting beliefs, which is why this writing can be so useful. So how do you define a happy childhood? It all depends on your perception of life and what yardstick you use to judge the degrees of joy, pain, love or sadness. In recent years, Mary made several trips to The Gambia in West Africa and although one of the poorest countries in the world, Mary found the people there some of the happiest, friendliest and peace loving she has ever met! Why were they so cheerful? *'Why not?'* one Gambian lady said, *'Why be miserable, it's not going to change anything?'*

Your perception of life is what's important. When settling in Canada, Mary briefly shared her life story with a new writing group. She told them how her childhood playground in England's post-war London was amongst the rubble on bombsites where houses, shops and offices once stood before being flattened to the ground. One member of the group, who grew up on a farm and enjoyed the freedom of the countryside, expressed horror at the revelation of such an upbringing. Mary saw it differently. She'd been told that the world was at war and imagined that all children played on bombsites and suffered the effects of sweet rationing (which to her was a much worse deprivation than the state of her playground). As George Orwell said *we didn't know how bad it was until they told us.*

Facts can't be changed although your understanding and perception of them can. If you have previously felt overwhelmed by events and circumstances, writing helps you gain a fresh perspective and rid yourself of unhelpful beliefs and emotions. The results, as countless people will testify, are well worth the effort. That is not to excuse another's behaviour or condone unpleasant actions but rather to understand that we are the people we are today in spite of (or maybe because of) those things.

Dave Pelzer, who suffered years of child abuse at the hands of his mother, says in his book, *A Man called Dave:*

> *I have lived through an extraordinary experience, yet I was fortunate enough to learn from it and walk away a better person. I can't change my past, and it does not grant me the right to use it as a crutch, nor am I destined to become a prisoner because of it. For years I have lived by the philosophy: that which does not kill you can only make you stronger.*

But don't take anyone else's word for it – it's time to start telling your story.

Where to Start?

This is an activity that Mary finds useful when conducting workshops. These six minutes of free intuitive writing gets your pen moving and your mind focused on expressing yourself without any inhibitions.

To help focus your mind, think about the following quote from Quentin Crisp:

> *An autobiography is an obituary in serial form with the last instalment missing.*

Before you begin, make sure you have plenty of time to spare and settle down somewhere quiet, preferably at a table or desk where you will be comfortable and undisturbed. Now write your own obituary with no holds barred – good things and not so good things. How would you like to be remembered by close family, friends and colleagues? What have been the important moments and events in your life?

Write for 6 minutes with an open heart and be totally honest, remember no one else will read your words.

Let your feelings and emotions flow through the pen onto the page as you write this portrait of why you are the person you are now.

Bring in the Family

The next stage of the exercise can follow on if you have the time available; otherwise wait until you have more time to yourself. First, find all the spare and odd buttons that you can, if you have an old-fashioned button box so much the better. If buttons aren't available, use mixed coins or currency of any denomination or tokens. Choose one button or coin to represent each member of your family, including yourself. Don't rush this. If you are using coins, chose ones of higher monetary value to represent those members of your family that you value the most. Think carefully about why you are choosing a particular button or coin. At a recent workshop, a student called Debbie chose a dull grey button with sharp triangular points, which she said symbolized her grandmother who had a cutting tongue and rarely smiled.

When you have chosen an item for everyone in your family, group the buttons or coins together to show how the relationship between all the members works, or doesn't, whatever the case may be. Debbie, mentioned above, felt her parents were controlling and so the tiny pearl button she'd chosen to represent her was obscured under the large buttons of her mother and father. Perhaps you feel that you don't or another family member doesn't fit in your family. If so, place the button or buttons outside the group.

Consider these buttons or coins and write a few paragraphs about your family dynamics and why you have put yourself in the position you have in the group.

Your Lifeline

Take a large sheet of paper and write your name in the centre at the top. Draw a line diagonally across the centre of the page from left to right as shown in the example. Put a marker at the beginning of the line and write the date of your birth here. The right hand end of the line denotes where you are today.

Use the writing from your 'obituary' and the group of buttons or coins as a guide, and mark off important events along your lifeline. Your first mark might denote the day you started school. Label this place with the number 1 and cross reference this event underneath. The second marker might denote learning to ride a bicycle – write the number 2 on the line and list the occurrence beneath the first milestone of starting school or whatever it happened to be. Don't worry about the dates of these events, simply place them on your line roughly where you think they fit and number them accordingly.

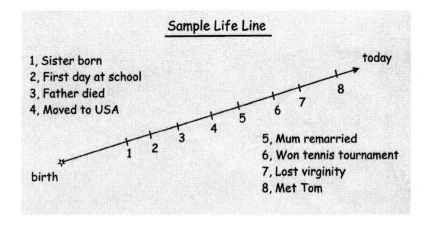

Sample Life Line

1, Sister born
2, First day at school
3, Father died
4, Moved to USA

today

5, Mum remarried
6, Won tennis tournament
7, Lost virginity
8, Met Tom

birth

Here are some memory joggers to help you compose your list:

- a memorable Christmas or birthday
- a birth or death in the family
- learning to skate or cycle
- an outing or holiday
- making a new friend
- losing an old friend
- going to a new school
- learning to swim
- doing exams
- first day at college
- first day at work
- first kiss
- a great (or dreadful) party
- losing your virginity
- getting hurt
- passing your driving test
- getting engaged
- getting married
- buying your first house
- getting promoted
- losing your job
- the birth of a child(ren)
- separation/divorce
- wedding anniversary

- losing control

- blind date

- health problem/operation

- moving house

- starting a new life

- a change of direction

- first day of retirement

Your First Instalment

Before you start the first instalment of your story place your completed lifeline and your six minutes of free intuitive writing in front of you. If you were inspired by the free writing exercise, you might like to carry on and finish more of your story in this way. That's OK. Otherwise choose one of the events in your lifeline, preferably one that stands out in your memory or an event that speaks to you. You'll know intuitively when this occurs and when it does pick up your pen and write about it. No self-censorship, no editing as you go, no concerns over writing, punctuation or spelling – just write! Initially, your memories may come as jumbled pieces of a jigsaw, so write what you feel and fill in the gaps using your imagination. Keep your button group in mind when doing this to get a more accurate picture of how family members interact.

Lytton Strachey said, *'Discretion is not the better part of biography.'* Don't worry about being tactful, be honest and write freely, expressing the emotions you felt at the time as well as the facts. Your story will come alive if you remember to include all the senses. Smell, for instance is a very potent one.

Let's say you are writing about your first day at school. Visualise the scene. Is your mother cooking bacon for breakfast or your father cooking porridge, as you get ready for your big day? And now you've arrived at school what can you see? Is the school bigger or smaller than you expected? Does this scare or excite you? Is it raining? Does the cloakroom have an aroma of damp, sweaty clothing? Does the hall smell of stinky feet and floor polish? Maybe your teacher smells pleasantly of lily-of-the-valley or unpleasantly of mothballs?

Describe your classroom – where are you sitting? And what about the sounds? Does the noise of other children frighten you? What other noises are there? Music pays a large part in many of our lives and often evokes vivid memories. Does your teacher play the piano and do you sing hymns or songs?

Also think about touch. Has someone given you a toy for comfort on your first day? Is it soft? Furry? Hard? Cold? Smooth? And finally, remember taste. Are you given school milk? Is it warm, cold, creamy, watery, disgusting? What about your school dinner? Is it delicious or unappetising? Light or stodgy? Undercooked, just right or does it have burned edges and undersides? Have you taken a packed lunch? Continue using all your senses to paint an evocative picture with your words.

Another's Viewpoint?

First part over, you now need to think about writing the same story from the point of view of another person who was involved. This can be particularly beneficial if you have written about a traumatic or confrontational incident involving a family member. Try writing the same scenario from their point of view. How did they feel and where were they coming from? See if you can make sense of why they acted the way they did. As said before, this is not designed to condone or excuse actions but to try and gain some understanding of them. Mary found this part of the exercise valuable in dealing with what she terms *some unsavoury childhood issues*.

But, for simplicity's sake, let's take our example above of writing about your first day at school. You could now choose to write the story from your mother's point of view, for example. Was she glad to see the back of you because you were bored and naughty before your first day? Or was she sad because you were growing up and leaving her? Even if you're not sure what the reality was, *imagine how she felt* based on what you know of her. How do you think her day shaped up when you disappeared from her life, however briefly? Write as much as you can from this opposing point of view and try to get into the other person's shoes, this will truly give you a greater understanding of the event.

Finally

What do you do with this writing? That is entirely up to you. Some of you may be inspired to write more accounts of your early years, building into later and more recent chapters of your life. If this is the case, you might like to put your first words away somewhere safe. After all you have written freely, unguarded. You've shared your hurts, joys, and innermost feelings and communicated, perhaps for the first time, events and details that have lived a long time locked inside. You might choose to take your writing out and reflect on it from time to time, or at a later stage do some editing and re-working until the piece is to your satisfaction. And, many people discover that having written their life and secrets out in this way the relief is so great they feel transformed. So much so they want to share what they've written. That's for you to decide, as this isn't what this book is about.

You can tear your work up into little pieces now and put it in the rubbish, put it through a shredder or place it in a bottle and throw it out to sea. There are all sorts of options here. You could keep it in your wallet or purse and carry it around. Mary found it useful to ritually burn her outpourings in a tin can, somewhere safe in the open and away from combustible materials. She would rip the pages up and ceremoniously drop them into the can while repeating, *I let go of the past, I let go of the past...* A match was thrown into the papers and Mary concentrated on watching them burn as she continued to repeat, *I let go of the past* ... over and over. She says she found this ritual purged her of many problems and hang-ups.

To quote the American teacher, Brendan Halpin:

> *When my wife was diagnosed with breast cancer, I joked that I couldn't decide between overeating and alcoholism as a copy strategy. My wife suggested I write about it instead. She is always right. I couldn't write a cloying sentimental story of inspiring courage so I wrote what was real to me – fear, lust, annoyance, love, fatigue, resentment, existential terror, horror movies, alcohol and country music. It's not pretty but it is real.*

Pick up a pen and write what's real to you. You'll find it cathartic and therapeutic. Some would say magical.

Future Magic

"I have seen the future and it works."

Lincoln Steffens

The aim here is to put you in the driving seat on your journey, your hands firmly on the steering wheel of life, looking ahead and rarely bothering with the rear view mirror!

Here you get to focus on the things that are most important to you. Following this, you write up a plan with the intention that the coming year is the best it can be for you personally and professionally. The process works best if you complete all the exercises in this chapter at one sitting so you need to set aside up to three hours somewhere restful and comfortable where you will not be disturbed. Your local library could be a good place if finding the necessary peace and quiet at home is difficult. Have lots of paper and pens available.

Step 1 – Your Life Chart

One of the most important aspects of a successful, contented life is balance, with an equal measure of everything that's important to you, such as work, family, leisure time and fun. Balance is often difficult to achieve in a world seemingly full of chaos, stress, frenetic schedules, commitments and demands on our energy and time. We have to remember that balance is not static, there is continual action either away from, towards or through balance and although we can slow the tempo, it is only when we leave this earthly plane that it stops altogether! Life is so busy it often appears we've become human doings instead of human beings. Completing the following Life Chart will reveal how balanced your life is at present.

You can use the blank chart in this book (using the sample as a guide) or copy your own version onto a piece of paper. If you feel some of the categories are not applicable to you and want to change them or add more, please do. You might choose to split *Family and Friends* into two separate categories, for example, or add a category for *Exercise* if this is important for you. This is your chart, your life! And date the chart too as this is all about how you feel today, right at this moment.

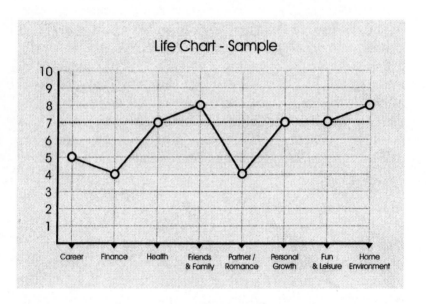

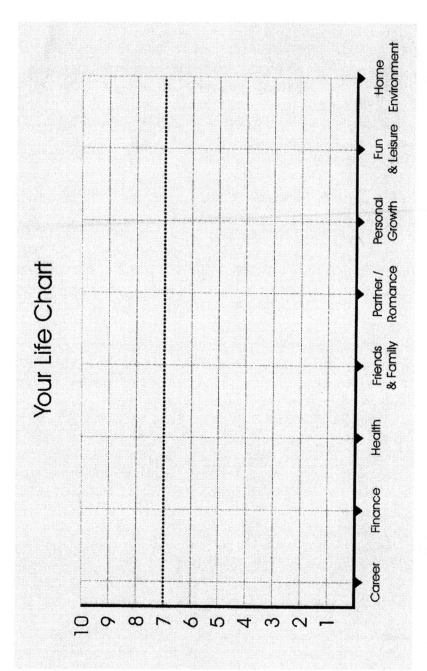

To complete your Life Chart you rate your level of satisfaction with each part of your life on a scale of zero to 10, with zero representing total dissatisfaction and 10 being total satisfaction, mark your chart as shown. And remember, this is about *your* satisfaction. You may have a disability, for example, which you consider a gift and are completely at ease with, so in this instance you might score high in the health section. Someone else could have a similar disability and consider their life blighted forever, in which case they would put a much lower score. The chart needs to be an honest visual indicator of how you feel.

Finished? How balanced is your chart? How balanced is your life? What peaks and troughs are there? What might you need to focus on for the coming year?

As a general guideline anything scoring seven and under will benefit from your attention. A score of over seven in any category is good news, but don't let complacency roost in your soul. Our sample chart shows career, finance and partner/romance requires thought for this person in the near future since they scored the lowest. It pays to look at their life as a whole however as they may need to communicate better to realise their career potential which in turn would have a positive impact on their finances. And better communication skills could be considered a personal growth issue.

When balance goes from our lives so does choice, or so it seems. In this condition we are driven by circumstances as though we don't have the power to choose. We say, *I must, I can't, I should* or we assign our power to a third party as though somebody else is pulling our strings... *I can't do that because he will be...* We need to give ourselves a new perspective and doing this exercise is a step in the right direction.

Step 2 – Your Accomplishments

What did you accomplish in the past year? Write down as many examples as you can think of however insignificant you consider them to be. Look at the sections of your Life Chart to help you and try to list at least one accomplishment for each segment.

Let's take *Family* for instance. Here you could list items as diverse as organising a Golden Wedding Anniversary party for your parents to having raised a teenage son single handed who still tells you (between moods) that he loves you. For remembering to put the rubbish out more often than not, to making regular telephone calls and visits to Uncle Billy. For giving your children's ideas much needed support to nursing your significant other through a serious illness. Be as comprehensive as possible and don't sell yourself short. Most of you will find you accomplished far more than you ever imagined. If you've had a difficult year, it's important to acknowledge and appreciate yourself so congratulate yourself on all you have achieved.

Here are some examples of things you may have accomplished:

- you learned a new skill
- you were promoted
- you ate healthier
- you quit smoking
- you moved house
- you started your own business
- you paid your credit card bills on time
- you decorated the lounge
- you stayed calm when your holiday flight was delayed
- you looked after your mum when she was poorly, and you still went to work
- you made more time for your children
- you gave yourself extra time and space
- you went on a self-development course
- you made a new friend
- you contacted an old friend and made a date

Step 3 – Your Challenges

James Joyce said, *Mistakes are the portals of discovery*.

Mistakes, disappointments, failures and problems equate to one thing in this book – challenges! So what were your biggest challenges of the last year? Be honest here and again use the sections of the chart as memory joggers. List as many occasions as possible where you didn't feel life came up to your expectations and also where you felt other people let you down. Recall all the instances you can think of, for example:

- did you have dreams that didn't come true?

- did you lose your focus?

- did you hope for a pay rise that didn't materialise?

- did you hope to find a new partner for life – and didn't?

- did you lose a loved one?

- did you go over the limit on your credit card?

- did you hope to return to further education – and didn't?

- did you hope to start a family – and it didn't happen?

- did you wish for a holiday in an exotic location that didn't materialise?

- did you have some health problems that set you back?

- did you put on weight?

- did you fall out with a friend or family member?

You may think that this is an exercise to be avoided especially if your list of challenges outweighs your list of achievements, but just tell yourself you've had several tests of your character over the last year. Besides, we don't believe in failure. Everything you do brings about a result. The result may not be the one you intended, but at least you know how not to achieve something!

Writing everything down does serve a purpose, if only to remind you how strong you are to have dealt with so much in such a short time. And ask yourself these questions:

Do you know of anyone who has *never* had any setbacks or challenges?

Do you know of anyone who accomplishes *every* goal they set?

The thing to remember here is: *You might not always feel you choose your challenges, but you do choose how you react to them.* And you can use these occasions to learn and grow. Acknowledge and face these challenges head-on because invariably you will find a reason for them later. Sometimes *much* later.

True Life Example

Here are some of the challenges that a client, Davina noted about the year 2001:

1) the frustration of listening to and watching a close friend repeat addictive behaviour

2) the cost of advertising not covering the funds Davina made from her new business venture

3) the slimming club going into liquidation nationally, forcing Davina to close her group.

4) having little success doing makeovers and selling cosmetics.

5) a close friendship with two males proved unsustainable.

So what did Davina learn from these challenges? Here's her list:

1) that you can't make people change, they have to want it for themselves and you can only support them in this

2) that throwing money into something doesn't guarantee success

3) the Slimming Club appeared to be a failure however she learned she could stand up in front of strangers and give a 20 minute talk

4) she should listen to herself and not be so impulsive. She knew deep down the cosmetics wouldn't work because she doesn't enjoy selling but she let herself be talked into signing up

5) a relationship with the opposite sex is no longer a priority in Davina's life

Now take each item on your list of challenges and write down what you think the lesson was, and if you learned from it? Be totally honest about your feelings here. If you don't feel you've learned anything from a particular instance, then say so. It doesn't mean you didn't, it simply means you can't see what it might be at this particular time. Think about why a challenge did or didn't work. In Davina's case, when she reflected on her new business venture, she realised that spending large sums of money on advertising doesn't necessarily mean clients will come flocking. She's learnt an enormous amount from this.

We can all be wise after the event, but would you do things differently if you had the last year over again? Your answer can give you a clue as to what you have learned from the situation. What new *basic truths* have you taken on board here that could give you guidance for the coming year? Try to come up with at least one statement relating to each of the different challenges you wrote down. For example, let's say you are a busy working parent and as one of your challenges you were asked to run the local youth club. There was no one else to take on this role and the club would close if you didn't comply. Reluctantly, you agreed to become a youth leader.

This extra responsibility made life more hectic and stressful than ever. What might your *basic truth* statement be in this case?

I will learn to say NO without attaching any guilt to the word or

I will increase my self- esteem so it's not necessary for me to behave like 'superman/superwoman' or

I will learn to make more time for myself or

I will learn to be true to my personal values and myself

To help you work these truths into your everyday way of being you need to rewrite them as affirmations, remembering to make them personal and positive. And to put them in the present – as if what you want is already here, such as:

I say no with ease

I am always true to myself and my values

Finished? Now you need to discover what your personal values are.

Step 4 – Your Values

The closer you live to your own personal values the more content you are and the more balanced your life. Values are who you *are*. They are those things you need in life and without which you live a life of tension and lack fulfilment, some might say die a little. Values differ for everyone. You might have a value of *structure* and *accuracy* in your life, whereas someone else's values might be *risk-taking* or *accomplishment*. You cannot select right or wrong values and no one value is better or worse than another. Don't select a value simply because you believe it sounds good or you feel it's the right value to have. This defeats the exercise and worst

94

of all, prevents you living the life you want, the life you are here to live.

Whatever your values are, being faithful to them consistently leads to a happier, more contented life. It is these hidden drives that get you out of bed in the morning, fire your ambition and fuel your determination to improve your life. Everyone can get excited and enjoy life when they live it in alignment with their values, although this may sometimes involve going through seemingly less happy times to honour your values. Once you do this however you emerge from the experience richly satisfied you acted in accordance with your values.

The more aware you become of these values, the more you empower yourself to make the changes necessary to have a more fulfilled life. Maybe you enjoy painting rugged landscapes, but painting isn't the value here. The value could be *nature, beauty* or *creativity*. Maybe you enjoy having holidays, but the holidays are not a value. The values here could be *adventure, fun* and *connection with others*. So what makes you tick?

Citing a list of values here as an example would be unproductive as people generally choose the most desirable or socially acceptable ones, whereas you need to be true to yourself. Making a list of values off the top of your head is no easy task, so you might need to write a few paragraphs about yourself and your belief system – a slice of life for today if you like. It could go something like this:

My name is Joe and one of my priorities at the moment is to start painting again *(values: creativity and self expression)* so I will rejoin the watercolour artists' group as I miss the sense of belonging *(value: participation)*. My other priority is to spend more time with the children *(value: love of family)*. I've also made the decision to give up my job and go freelance as an insurance consultant from February *(values: accomplishment* and *courage)*. I only need to give my boss a month's notice, but I'm going to let him know in the next few days as I know how difficult it's going to be to replace me *(values: integrity* and *lack of pretence).* I was pleased today when Susie asked me to go walking with her in the dales. I love being with her on walks *(values: connectedness).* She can be such great fun *(values: lightness)* and she is always so good at telling me what I'm good at *(value: acknowledgement).* All in all, although I've got a lot of challenges and things I want to achieve *(values: accomplishment)* I feel excited by the prospect.

From the paragraph you write, you should be able to draw up a list of values but please add any others you can think of that aren't in your slice of life. Looking at the above, Joe's list would read like this: *creativity, self expression, participation, love of family, accomplishment, courage, integrity, lack of pretence, connectedness, lightness, acknowledgement* and *accomplishment.*

Don't get hung up on words either, use the words which have meaning for you. If you'd written the above slice of life you might have chosen to write *independence* instead of *courage, honesty* instead of *integrity, friendship* instead of *participation.* All that matters is that *you* know what you mean by the word you choose.

Ideally you need to find at least 10 values that are important to you. When you have, make a fresh list noting them in the order of importance to you with the most important being at the top of your list to the least important being at the bottom. Joe's list might read:

1. *Accomplishment*

2. *Love of family*

3. *Self expression*

4. *Creativity*

5. *Acknowledgement*

6. *Participation*

7. *Integrity*

8. *Lack of pretence*

9. *Connectedness*

10. *Lightness*

When you have a list of values in order of preference, move onto the next section.

Step 5 – Your Goals

Have another look at your Life Chart and decide which area you would like to make your main focus for the coming year? The obvious answer would be the category that scored the lowest points on your assessment but any area you feel drawn to concentrate on is good – follow your intuition here.

Thinking about this aspect of your life, what you would need to do to raise your score by just one point? Don't forget about your values list and your basic truth statements as you consider this question. Let's assume that you've chosen the area *Significant other/Romance* as your primary focus and on your Life Chart this scored four points only. What would you need to do or have happen so you could rate this area of your life a five? What would it be like if it rated a 10?

Why has it only scored four? Have you been too busy with your career and are always tired when you come home? Is this why you haven't made any effort with regard to relationships recently? To increase your rating, the answer might be to start going out more and to meet different groups of people. How will you do this? Write plenty of ideas out here and keep writing however silly some of the ideas might seem. And don't attach yourself to any of them at this stage as being right or wrong for you – simply look at what you could do. Put your ideas in the form of an empowering statement to say, for example: *I attract someone who fits and empowers me* or *I open my heart and invite others into my life*. Either of these statements could be your primary goal. How will you achieve this primary goal?

Now move onto the other categories of the Life Chart and think about how you can increase your score in each section by at least one point. Then write a statement that can be your goal for this particular area. Perhaps you rated *Health* six and in order to score seven you need to exercise more. If so, you could make your health goal statement, *I set aside time for myself to go to dancing classes.*

Maybe in the *Personal Growth* section your score of five could be increased by doing some self-development workshops. Your statement could read: *I deepen my commitment to spiritual practice.* If you are fortunate enough to have scored the maximum 10 points in any area write a statement congratulating yourself! And consider how you'll maintain this score. When you have completed all sections of the Life Chart use these statements to make a list of goals starting with your primary focus.

Finished? Take copies or type up this list and keep it somewhere safe where you can look at it frequently, perhaps in your in-tray at work, on your bedside table or in the magazine rack or your briefcase. Look at it regularly to help you stay focused. Decide weekly which area needs your attention and have a goal or intention for each week and month. You might choose to join a lunch club at work in the first month, find out about fitness classes in your area during the second month and arrange to go on a retreat in the third. Remember to focus and act in alignment with your values as well as the tasks you set yourself.

The Magic

There's something we need to tell you at this point and it's this: there is something about the very act of writing your goals down, seeing them there on the page in front of you, which speaks to you on some level. It says: 'Aha, so that's what you want.' And somehow, somewhen, the goals become realised. So if you go through nothing more than the above exercise and come up with a list of goals which you then put in a knickers or sock drawer only to rediscover it in a year or two's time – some will have happened, believe us. We know this, it's happened to us and numerous other people. Why? *Because, quite simply, that is the magic of writing things down!*

Sallyann Sheridan and Mary Wood run workshops and courses based on *The Magic of Writing Things Down* in Canada and Europe for companies, charities, support groups and individuals. If you'd like to attend a workshop or simply want further details, please email Sallyann at:

sallyann@sallyannsheridan.com or visit
www.sallyannsheridan.com

We'd love to hear from you.